Long Journey South

Dawn McMillan
Illustrated by Tanya Cooper

Pearson Australia
(a division of Pearson Australia Group Pty Ltd)
707 Collins Street, Melbourne, Victoria 3008
PO Box 23360, Melbourne, Victoria 8012
www.pearson.com.au

First published 2014 by Pearson Australia
2018 2017 2016
10 9 8 7 6 5 4 3 2

Publisher: Dian Faulisi
Project Managers: Tamara Pirois and Rachel Davis
Editor: Johanna Rohan
Cover and series designer: Jenny Grigg
Designers: Jennifer Johnston and Nina Heryanto
Copyright & Pictures Editor: Katy Murenu
Mac Operator: Rob Curulli
Cover art: Tanya Cooper
Illustrator: Tanya Cooper
Printed in Australia by the SOS Print - Media Group

ISBN 978 1 4860 0750 9

Pearson Australia Group Pty Ltd ABN 40 004 245 943

Disclaimer
Some of the images used in *Long Journey South* might have associations with deceased Indigenous Australians. Please be aware that these images might cause sadness or distress in Aboriginal or Torres Strait Islander communities.

Contents

Chapter 1

Cornwall, England, 1848

Edward breathed in the smell of the potatoes and turnips as they bubbled in the big pot hanging over the fire. He was sure that the vegetables were cooked, but his mother was in no hurry to serve dinner.

She was sitting at the table, her head in her hands. There was a letter on the table. Edward wondered if it was bad news. Perhaps Uncle Albert had died. He'd gone to Australia a few years ago, to work in the copper mines.

"Mother," Edward whispered, "is the letter about Uncle Albert? Is he all right?"

"Yes, Edward. All is well with Albert," his mother said. "There's no need for you to worry. Now let's be having our dinner."

And with that she folded the letter and put it in her skirt pocket. "Call the others," she said. "And see if there is any bread left in the safe, will you?"

2 July, 1848

Mother didn't say much to me at dinner tonight. She hasn't shown me the letter yet, but I think she has shown the others. They're all in the kitchen, talking in hushed voices. I can't make out what they're saying but they sound excited.

Now, I can hear Uncle John's voice, rising above the others. I hear him say, "You lot please yourselves," and I wonder what is going on ...

Cornwall, England, 1848

When Edward awoke, his brother and uncles had already left for work at the mine. As he ate his gruel for breakfast, his mother said, “We might be going to Australia, son.”

“Australia!’ gasped Edward.

“Soon, there’ll be no work for your brother and uncles in the mines here,” said his mother. “In his letter, Uncle Albert said there’s plenty of work in Australia. There are copper mines down in the south.”

"Your brother's keen to go, and his Mary, too," continued his mother. Uncle George and Aunt Lily think it's a wonderful idea."

"Uncle John?" Edward asked.

"He's not sure he wants to go," his mother answered.

Edward felt his heart sink. He didn't want to leave Uncle John behind. But at the same time, he was excited.

Australia! A sailing ship! A big adventure!

2 September, 1848

We are going to Australia! Our family has just been accepted as government-assisted immigrants. My brother, Davey, and Uncle George will be working at the mines in Burra Burra, in South Australia!

We'll be sailing on the ship the *William Money*. Uncle George says the *William Money* is a wooden ship with three masts, called a barque. I wonder if it will be safe if there's a big storm ...

There's been lots of talk in the village about the voyage. I've heard people talking about the diseases you can get on a ship. I'm a bit scared, but I won't let Mother know. When Father died, I promised I'd take care of her.

The first thing we must do is get to Plymouth, where the ship is. It'll be a long journey to get there.

Uncle John's coming to Plymouth with us, but just to say goodbye. I wish he was coming to Australia, too.

Chapter 2

Setting sail

16 September, 1848

We've made it to Plymouth, at last. It took a whole week to get here! The roads were so bumpy and rough. I had to walk a lot of the way because there weren't enough wagons for everyone. The women, the young children and the luggage travelled in the wagons, and the men walked.

We have to stay in a government emigration depot until we leave. The depot is actually an old warehouse, separated into dormitories.

There are about seventy people sleeping in my dormitory! My bed isn't very clean. I wonder who has slept here before me ... I'll try not to think about it! I'll just think of the big adventure that awaits us.

We'll be boarding the ship, and leaving England in three days. Three days! I'm feeling a bit confused. Part of me wants to jump on board and sail away to Australia, but the other part of me wants to go home to Cornwall.

Edward watched as the long boats were rowed back and forth to the *William Money*. Some were piled high with trunks, boxes and suitcases – others loaded with people, ready to climb aboard the ship.

When it was his family's turn, Edward's heart missed a beat. He choked back his tears as Uncle John held him tightly. Then, his mother hugged her brother.

"Off you go, then," said Uncle John, holding his hat to his chest. "Get on that ship – the lot of you! And the best of luck to you all!" he said as Edward led his mother away to the long boat.

Edward struggled for breath as he turned his head to have one last look at Uncle John. He might never see his uncle again. He was very, very sad.

The ship moved beneath Edward's feet as he stepped on board. Edward looked around him, up and down the deck. What looked like a big ship from the dock now seemed so small. How would it carry 372 passengers, as well as the crew, on such a long voyage? He guessed that the deck was only about twelve or thirteen paces across.

Suddenly, Uncle George called him to go below deck. Edward was relieved to find that their family had a space below deck to call their own. If he'd been older he would have had to be with the men, in the forepart of the ship. Yes, he was glad they were all together. His mother needed him to be with her.

Edward made his way back up on deck. He and his family watched the last of the passengers board. The deck was getting crowded.

“Mother!” Edward called. “Uncle George! Aunt Lily! Davey! Mary! Quick! We need to be by the rail. Hurry! Uncle John will be looking out for us!”

At five o’clock the air cracked with the sound of the ship’s horn. Edward felt the ship tremble as it started to move. He waved to Uncle John, somewhere in the crowd. Finally, they were on their way to Australia!

19 September, 1848

I'm writing this up on deck. Uncle George said the ship's charter states that each passenger must have space on deck. So here I am, sitting in my 'deck space!'

He also told me that aboard the ship there would be bunks, tables and chairs, and even a space on deck for a school with desks. A school! I don't want to go to school on a trip like this. I'm far too old for school anyway. When we get to Australia, I'm going to get a job, although Mother doesn't want me working in the copper mines. She thinks I'm too young for that.

It's nice to be up on deck with some fresh air and space. There's no room to move below deck. The bunks are so close together and Mother is trying to get our things organised. Uncle Davey is sleeping on the top bunk. I know how loudly he snores and I wonder if I'll get any sleep!

We're far away from shore now. The tugboats are ready to let us go. One last blast of each tugboats' horn and the ropes are gone. The ship's masts are gleaming in the late afternoon sun as we head out to sea.

I'm going to stop writing now. I want to watch as the sails go up and the ship picks up speed.

Chapter 3

First days at sea

To begin with, the weather was fair. Even so, Edward found it hard to get used to the motion of the ship. His stomach felt queasy and his head ached. Uncle George was queasy, too. "If we're like this now, boy," he said to Edward, "we'll be a right mess if it gets really rough."

But surprisingly, when the weather turned bad, Edward found that both he and Uncle George felt better. "The swell of the sea made us queasy," Uncle George explained. "The choppy sea has a different motion."

Edward's mother was fine. But Aunt Lily and Mary weren't so lucky. Lily was vomiting. Everyone was very worried as she was going to have a baby soon. Mary was as white as a ghost, and Davey stayed by her side.

23 September, 1848

What a night! Yesterday was bad enough, but last night was worse than anyone could imagine. A strong breeze blew fiercely and made the ship race along – so fast.

No one was talking much, but I did hear some people say that they might not make it to Australia. I was worried about Aunt Lily and Mary. Mother and I brought them water to drink and Uncle George talked to them to try and calm them down. Davey was busy pretending that he felt all right.

As I lay down in my bunk, I felt as if I was being tossed around like a cork in a barrel. It was too hard to sleep because of all the moaning and groaning from the passengers around us. Lots of people began to pray and some girls were crying. Mother's new friend, Mrs Menzies, was very worried about her sick baby.

I found out this morning, that some of the sailors were washed out of their bunks! The waves washed over the deck, through the hatches and into the sailors' quarters.

But this morning the weather has improved. There's still a strong wind but the sea is calmer. Mrs Menzies' baby seems a little better, too. And the good news is I've made a new friend. I just started talking to him, up on deck this morning. His name is Jimmy. He's one year younger than me, but he's tall so we look about the same age.

27 September, 1848

Today is the most amazing day! There's not much wind and it's warm. The children are up on deck for their school lessons. The women are doing their washing in the large tubs and hanging it on the clothes lines. I never imagined a ship with clothes lines.

There's talk that we'll be able to see land today. The captain showed us a map, and we're off the coast of Portugal. Soon, we should be able to see the Madeira Islands. I had never heard of Portugal until the captain showed it to me on the map.

Jimmy and I have just finished playing cards. We're sitting at the ship's stern. Jimmy is watching the sailors work, while I write in my diary. We're not going to worry about looking for land ourselves. There'll be plenty of shouting from everyone else to let us know when the islands are in sight.

Chapter 4

Waiting for the breeze

Four weeks into the journey, the wind dropped. Edward and Jimmy stood at the ship's rail and watched the calm sea. They were waiting to see the fish that Davey had told them about.

"Albacore," Davey said. "It's a tuna, a long-finned fish." Edward wondered how Davey knew such things, but he guessed that he'd been talking to the sailors.

Today, it was very hot. Many of the sailors were fishing. Edward was excited.

He thought that fresh fish would make a nice change from mutton and potatoes and soup. There wasn't much else to eat.

Suddenly, Jimmy shouted, "There's one! It's jumping out of the water!" Edward scanned the sea but he saw nothing.

But then, he saw four or five silver fish leaping out of the water together.

"Now I see them!" Edward called. "I hope the sailors catch some!"

17 October, 1848

It was stifling hot today. Everybody lazed around, except for the sailors who caught more fish. Mother and Aunt Lily sat on the shady side of the ship. Mary slept all afternoon.

There was not a breath of wind. I think the captain is getting worried about the ship not moving. Jimmy said that sometimes sailors have to row the life boats and tow ships to the wind. I'm not sure that's true. It might just be a story. But I wonder what will happen to our ship if the sea stays calm for too long.

The fish tasted great tonight. The crew cut it up into small pieces, so everyone could have some. It would be great if the sailors caught fish every day! Or maybe not, because that would mean the sea had to remain calm. I hope the wind comes up soon.

Looking for fish and birds has become a fun pastime for us while we wait for the wind. Davey is the best at spotting fish in the water. The children gather around him and scan the sea trying to spot the fish before he does. Davey always sees them first but sometimes he pretends to let us think we did. Jimmy's father can name many of the different kinds of birds we've seen. There are sea birds of course, and we've also seen swallows flying above the ship.

Jimmy's little cousin was the first to see a turtle! She squealed with delight and everyone rushed to take a look. I saw it just before it dived deep underwater. And then, there was more excitement from the starboard side of the ship. I peered over the edge and saw them – a pod of dolphins! They were swimming alongside the ship and leaping out of the water!

Edward thought there could be nothing more spectacular than seeing dolphins, until he saw the flying fish. The captain explained that their streamlined shape allowed them to build up speed under water until they broke through the surface. And then, their amazing wing-like fins kept them airborne.

"Wow!" gasped Edward, as he watched one fish fly through the air for over 30 seconds.

Although Edward wanted the wind to fill the sails, so the ship would move, he would be sad to leave these magic of the calm waters.

Chapter 5

Across the equator

With the wind picking up, and a faster speed of 8 knots, the *William Money* crossed the equator. The captain explained that in about two to three weeks, they would be sailing around the most southern tip of Africa, the Cape of Good Hope.

"Then it's a straight run to Australia!" Edward exclaimed. The captain shook his head.

"There's a long way to go yet, lad," he said. "Such a lot can happen on a journey like this."

25 October, 1848

Today has been hard. Everyone was happy when we crossed the equator, but now so many people are sick with fever and dysentery. Mother is feeling very poorly and I'm worried about her – she never gets sick. And Aunt Lily is going to have her baby soon. What if she gets sick as well?

Jimmy's little sister is also running a high temperature. Jimmy is washing her with a cold cloth to try to keep her cool. I hope she will be all right. People have already died on board from dysentery – even one of the sailors. We all stood on deck as his body was lowered to the sea.

Davey says it's no wonder so many people are sick. The living conditions are so cramped. We can't keep ourselves very clean. And, when the weather is rough and the hatches are battened down, we can't get to the water closets. The smells are awful then.

When I see the sick people, I hope and pray that our family will be all right. But we are strong and I keep imagining that we all arrive in Australia together – fit and healthy.

8 November, 1848

Mother is missing home so much. I found her near the bow of the ship this morning. She was crying. I sat with her. I told her how amazing it was going to be to see Uncle Albert after such a long time, and to finally arrive in Australia.

I reminded her about Uncle Albert's letter. He said that there were new cottages being built in Burra Burra. He told us about the cave houses already there, built into the banks. I thought that living in a cave house would be fun. Mother says any house would be better than the ship, but I know she really wants a cottage.

She cheered up when I told her that we were only about a week away from the Cape of Good Hope, and in another seven weeks we should be landing in Australia!

I copied the captain's map and I'm trying to keep track of where we are. I hope my calculations are correct ...

Chapter 6

Heading south

It was bitterly cold the day that the *William Money* passed the Cape of Good Hope, south of Africa. The sea was heavy and a fog hung over the ship. The deck was slippery and Edward watched in horror as Jimmy slipped and fell backwards, landing with a thud.

Jimmy screamed as his arm twisted under him. When he sat up Edward could see that his arm was broken. "Your arm!" he said as he rushed to Jimmy's side. "It's all crooked!"

14 November, 1848

What a day! This morning Jimmy broke his arm. He was in a lot of pain. The ship's surgeon put his arm in a splint, and then a sling. He gave him something for the pain, and he's been sleeping most of the day. I hope he's feeling better tomorrow.

We're now in the Indian Ocean. I look at my map and it's almost a straight line to Australia.

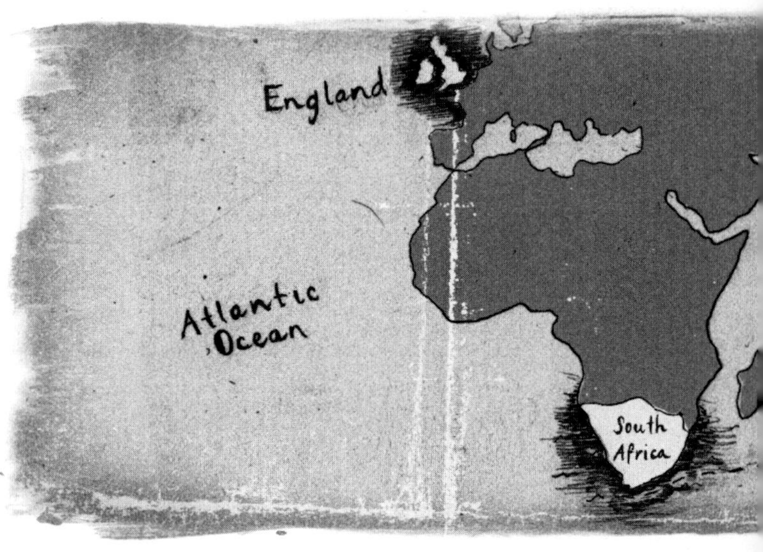

This afternoon the captain told us to look out for albatrosses, cape hens and cape pigeons. The captain says they are often seen around here. I hope we do see some. That will cheer Jimmy up.

Mother is feeling better now. She is excited about Aunt Lily's baby. The baby might be born on the ship! Aunt Lily is pleased that the worst of the sea sickness is over.

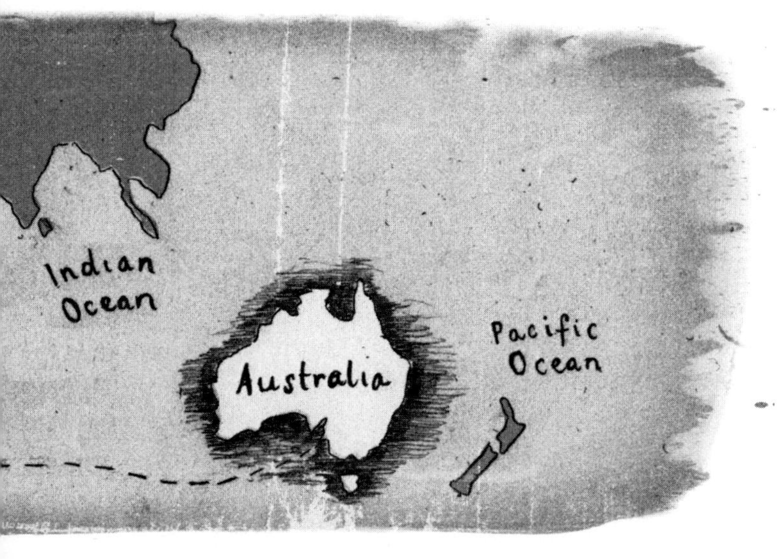

The weather warmed up as the *William Money* sailed across the vast Indian Ocean. On deck, Edward and Jimmy held their noses. There was a dreadful smell wafting over the ship.

"What is that smell?" exclaimed Jimmy.

"Dead sheep," explained Uncle George. "They need to throw them overboard before everyone's sick again!"

"No more mutton for dinner," added Davey. Edward felt his stomach churn. He wasn't sure if it was churning because of the thought of the chewy, salted mutton or at the thought of no meat at all.

"Perhaps someone will catch a shark and we can eat that for dinner," Davey went on. Edward felt better when he thought of fresh fish for dinner.

"Whales! Whales!" shouted someone from the port side of the ship. Edward and Jimmy rushed over to look at the whales. They watched as their sleek black humps surged through the water. They were glad to have something so amazing to take their minds off the terrible smell of the sheep.

12 December, 1848

I thought we might have good weather all the way to Australia, but I was wrong. Three days ago, a terrible storm hit us, and we've been below deck until now. The sea was so rough – the roughest sea since we left England.

A lot of people were seasick. Water came rushing down the hatches and flooded everything. All of our things are so wet – even the pages of my diary.

But today, the sun is shining, and we are drying everything up on deck. My diary is nearly dry and it's fine to write in now. Jimmy and I have been playing cards in the warm sun.

Mother, Davey and Mary are dancing with some of the other passengers. Jimmy and I are laughing at Davey. He keeps tripping up. Aunt Lily is sitting quietly. Her baby is due any day now, and Uncle George is keeping her company on deck.

Chapter 7

Australia, ahoy!

28 December, 1848

There is some exciting news today! I have a cousin! Aunt Lily had her baby – a wee boy, 'James William'. He is named James after my father, and William after the ship. James and Aunt Lily are both very well.

We are so close to Australia, I think my little cousin might be the first Australian in our family. The captain says we are only a few days away from docking the ship in Adelaide. We're travelling at a speed of 10 knots now! Soon, our long voyage will be over.

Edward and Jimmy leaned against the ship's rail, searching the horizon for land. "There! Can you see it, Edward?" Jimmy gasped.

Edward squinted his eyes against the glare of the sun on the sea. He could just make out some land. "Australia!" Edward shouted.

"That's Kangaroo Island!" the sailors called out.

"And Cape Jervis," pointed the captain.

"Look, Edward. We have an escort," laughed Edward's mother. She pointed down to the dolphins swimming alongside the ship. "It's a sign," she said. "Life's going to be good in Australia!"

Just off Holdfast Bay, a pilot came aboard the ship. He helped the captain navigate the *William Money* along the river until it dropped anchor at Port Adelaide.

They had arrived in Australia. Their long sea voyage was finally over.

4 January, 1849

We're here – finally! I can't believe it! We have arrived in Adelaide, our first stop in Australia. It's strange, but good, to walk on dry land again. I still feel like I'm on the ship though – like the ground is slowly rocking.

A new year and a new life – that's what Mother said today as the ship anchored at Port Adelaide. I think our new life is going to be great!

I keep forgetting that our journey isn't over yet ... We still have to travel around 100 miles to get to Burra Burra. But this time we'll be on dry land! I bet Uncle Albert will be so excited to see us. I can't wait to see him.

Uncle George says it will be a long, hard journey to Burra Burra. We'll be travelling by dray and bullock, and he says the road will be rough and dusty. But I don't care. I'm so excited to nearly be at our destination after so long.

And, what is really exciting is that Jimmy and his family will be living in Burra Burra, too! A new life to share with a new friend – I can't wait!